Dedicated To:
My students

Written By: Abigail Gartland

Hello, my name is St. Gianna Molla!

I was born in Italy in 1922.

As I grew up, my faith continued to be important to me. When I was 20 years old, I decided to study medicine.

After a few years, I met a man named Pietro. We fell in love and were married.

We loved each other so much, and we were blessed with three beautiful children.

Our little family was so perfect, and we found out we were expecting another baby!

We were so excited to welcome a fourth child, but one day, I felt very sick.

The doctor told me that my baby was sick, too.

The doctor told me that the baby was not going to live unless I had a very dangerous surgery.

I prayed to Jesus and asked Him to save my baby. I was still very sick, but my prayers were answered.

I did not survive, but my baby lived! I watched over my baby and the rest of my family from Heaven with Jesus and Mary.

Do you want to be more like me?

You can celebrate my feast day with me on April 28th.

I am the patron saint of moms and unborn children.

I pray for you every day of your life.

St. Gianna Molla pray for us!

opyright:

part: © PentoolPixie © LimeandKiwiDesigns
ensed purchased: 1/10/2024

About the Author
Abigail Gartland

I love the saints and I love my faith. The idea for sharing the stories of the saints with little ones came when my dear friends were expecting their first baby. I wanted to create something as unique and special as our friendship. Each book is dedicated to very special people and groups who have enriched my faith in different ways. I am blessed to write these stories and appreciate the unending support of my family and friends. When I am not writing, am a middle school teacher. I hope you enjoy these stories. I pray for each and every person who opens one of my books to learn more about the saints.

Abbie

www.ingramcontent.com/pod-product-compliance
Lightning Source LLC
LaVergne TN
LVHW051043070526
838201LV00067B/4899